The wind screamed into Balto's face, but he did not turn from it...

Instead, he strained forward, and the dogs behind him followed his example. Balto breathed in snow along with the bitter wind, but he only pulled harder.

Kaasen was relieved. He was completely lost, but Balto was not. Though by now Kaasen could not even see the lead dog through the thick, blowing snow, he could feel how confidently Balto was pulling. With every step, Balto was sending his musher a message—*Trust me. I'll get us home.*

Balto
— and the —
Great Race

by Elizabeth Cody Kimmel
illustrated by Nora Köerber

A STEPPING STONE BOOK™
Random House 🏠 New York

*Grateful acknowledgment is made to
Stephen Misencik, Jan McKay, and
Joanne Coburn of the Cleveland
Museum of Natural History.*

Text copyright © 1999 by Elizabeth Cody Kimmel. Illustrations copyright
© 1999 by Nora Köerber. All rights reserved under International and
Pan-American Copyright Conventions. Published in the United States by
Random House Children's Books, a division of Random House, Inc., New York,
and simultaneously in Canada by Random House of Canada Limited, Toronto.

www.randomhouse.com/kids

Library of Congress Cataloging-in-Publication Data
Kimmel, Elizabeth Cody.
Balto and the great race / by Elizabeth Cody Kimmel; illustrated by Nora
Köerber.
    p.   cm.   "A Stepping Stone Book."
SUMMARY: Recounts how the sled dog Balto saved Nome, Alaska, in 1925 from
a diphtheria epidemic by delivering medicine through a raging snowstorm.
ISBN 0-679-89198-6 (pbk.) — ISBN 0-679-99198-0 (lib. bdg.)
1. Balto (Dog)—Juvenile literature. 2. Sled dogs—Alaska—Nome—
Biography—Juvenile literature. 3. Diphtheria—Alaska—Nome—Prevention—
Juvenile literature. [1. Balto (Dog). 2. Sled dogs. 3. Dogs.] I. Köerber, Nora, ill.
II. Title. SF428.7.K55 1999 636.73—dc21 98-35753

Printed in the United States of America 19 18

For Shelly, Marcia, and Linda

CONTENTS

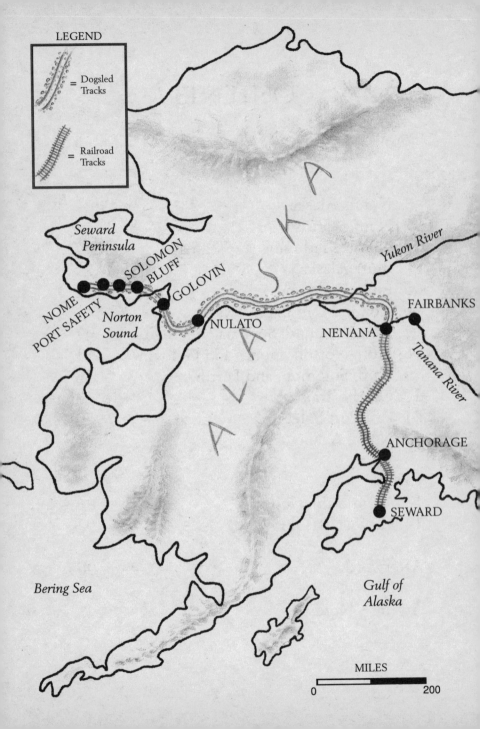

LEGEND

= Dogsled Tracks

= Railroad Tracks

Seward Peninsula

SOLOMON

BLUFF

GOLOVIN

NOME

PORT SAFETY

Norton Sound

NULATO

Yukon River

FAIRBANKS

NENANA

Tanana River

ALASKA

ANCHORAGE

SEWARD

Bering Sea

Gulf of Alaska

MILES

0   200

The medicine is transported by train from Anchorage to Nenana, the end of the line, over 650 miles from Nome.

Mushers lash the serum down for the dogsled journey across Alaska.

Balto waits in Bluff to take the serum home to Nome!

In Nome's tiny hospital, Dr. Welch and Nurse Morgan anxiously await the arrival of the life-saving serum.

HOSPITAL

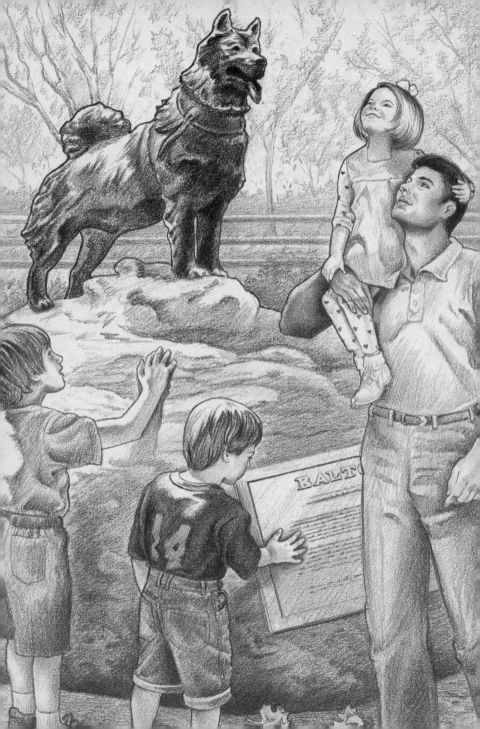

FOREWORD

Deep in the heart of Central Park, in New York City, stands a lone statue of a dog.

His head is up. His chest is barrel-strong. His tail is curled with pride. Whether blanketed with a soft coat of snow or hot to the touch from the rays of the summer sun, the statue gives off a great feeling of power, accomplishment, and strength.

People walking along the path slow down as they come upon the statue. They stop and look up at his strong muzzle and powerful paws.

1

Who is this dog?

A plaque at the base of the statue tells people a little. The dog's name is Balto. He was a Siberian husky. His hometown was Nome, Alaska. The last three words on the plaque are:

ENDURANCE—FIDELITY—INTELLIGENCE

Looking from these words back to the silent, wise face of Balto, one wants to know more. Who was Balto? Why is he remembered and talked about to this very day? And what could a dog from Alaska have done to deserve a statue in New York City?

The answers to these questions make up a story worth telling and retelling. A wonderful story. A true one.

To find out about Balto, we must turn back the clock to the year 1925 and travel to Nome, Alaska.

PART 1

CHAPTER ONE
Nome, Alaska

Nome began as a frontier town in 1899 when gold was discovered nearby. Once the gold ran out, most of the people left too. Even today, there are no roads linking Nome to the rest of the state.

Alaska became a state in 1959. It is one of the largest states, but it has fewer people in it than almost any other state in the country. Outside the big towns and cities, houses may be hundreds of miles away from each other.

The year 1925 was a good one to be a dog in Nome, Alaska. There were many opportunities for a strong canine with powerful legs and a healthy set of lungs.

Racing dogs could pull their sleds clear across the state, through some of the most beautiful—and deadly—landscape in the world. Every Alaskan dog with a breath of life in him dreamed of running the great northern sled races.

Purebred malamutes and Siberian huskies, like Balto, were the sled drivers' breeds of choice. But even a dog who was a mutt mix of eight breeds could be a sled dog. Sled drivers, known as *mushers*, could look at a dog and know in an instant if he was a natural for a team. And a dog with the right personality and skills could be chosen to lead a team.

The world of dog racing is one of

rivalry and competition. Even today it is a favorite sport in Alaska.

In addition to running in the dog races, which were held in the winters, many dog teams worked with local mining companies. They carried men and supplies where they were needed. The Northern Commercial Company even had a system of dog teams to carry and deliver mail throughout Alaska.

Balto's owner was Leonhard Seppala. He trained sled dogs and worked with his dog teams for the Hammon Consolidated Gold Fields Company. For men like Seppala, working for the company was simply something to do between dog races.

Seppala and his dogs had run almost every dog race organized in Alaska. They won again and again. Seppala's team held the record for the fastest time running from the town of Nenana to the city of Nome.

In putting together his racing team, Seppala used his favored breed—the Siberian husky. Seppala always tried to convince the mushers at the Nome Kennel Club that the Siberian was a superior breed and a faster racer. The breed could be traced back over two thousand years to Siberia, which lies across the Bering Sea from Alaska.

After hundreds of generations working with people as guard and work dogs, Siberian huskies have become a gentle breed. They are known for their great devotion to their owners.

One of Seppala's favorite dogs—a Siberian husky, of course—was named Togo. When Togo was just a puppy, he had broken free from his pen and followed

Seppala as he set off on a trip one night. The team was thirty miles into the wilderness before Seppala realized that the puppy had followed him. Unable to turn back, Seppala harnessed the eager pup to the rest of his dog team.

As young as he was, Togo showed himself to be a talented lead dog. From that day forward, he was a highly prized member of Seppala's team.

Balto and Togo were both trained by Seppala, but Balto often ran with another team of dogs that was owned by a man in Nome named Gunnar Kaasen. Kaasen was a very good friend of Seppala's. The two men had an agreement that Kaasen could borrow Balto whenever he needed him.

This agreement was about to make a difference to a lot of people.

CHAPTER TWO
Nome: Crisis!

In January 1925, winter settled over Alaska like an iron blanket. There were snowdrifts, high winds, and blizzards. Temperatures often dropped as low as thirty or forty degrees below zero.

Once winter came, the people of Nome were totally cut off from the outside world. But that January of 1925, a crisis came to the small, isolated city, and even the toughest citizens knew they needed help—winter or not.

The crisis was a diphtheria epidemic. An *epidemic* is the very quick spread of a disease to a large number of people. Epidemics can be very difficult to stop, even under good conditions. And the conditions in Nome were far from good.

Diphtheria, which often struck children in the past, begins with a flu-like fever and a sore throat. The disease quickly progresses to a very serious stage and is often deadly. Today, children are given a simple injection to prevent them from catching the disease, but in 1925 the only cure was an *antitoxin serum*.

In Nome, there was just enough serum to treat a few infected people. Without it, many people would die.

Dr. Curtis Welch was the sole doctor in all of Nome. He knew he had to get help!

There were no telephones in Nome, so Dr. Welch sent out an urgent plea for help by telegraph. Soon, all of America was waiting and listening for word of the sick and snowbound Alaskans.

A large supply of the antitoxin serum was found on the other side of Alaska in a city called Anchorage. The medicine was transported by train to the town of Nenana. That was as far north and west as the railroad tracks went.

Nenana was still quite a ways from Nome—650 miles! With winter at its worst, there were no passable roads out of Nenana. And the two local airplanes, which made summer flights, were unusable. As Dr. Welch tried frantically to help his patients, the situation grew worse and worse.

How could the serum get to Nome in time?

The workers of the Northern Commercial Company—the mining company that used dog teams for its mail system—had an idea. They thought that their mail system was the answer to the problem of transporting the serum.

The Northern Commercial mail system worked like this: the mail traveled a variety of paths and was transferred from dogsled to dogsled until it reached its destination. The sleds ran frequently, and the paths were well known to the dogs and mushers alike. Even in January's severe weather conditions, an experienced musher and team could travel the mail routes.

The biggest problem was timing. A package dropped off at the train station in Nenana usually took about a month to arrive in Nome by dogsled.

Many people in Nome were already infected with diphtheria, and more were coming down with it every day. Most of the sick people were children. A month was simply too long for them to wait. The medicine had to reach them much more quickly.

The Northern Commercial Company did not waste a minute.

All over Alaska, the very best mushers and those with the strongest and fastest dogs volunteered. The idea was to set up a giant relay course across the state. If enough drivers and dogs were ready and waiting, the precious cargo could travel from one sled to the next without stopping for more than a moment!

Almost every town had a musher who wanted to join the relay. For a driver and team to run their best, each team could cover only a short distance. A tired and overworked team would slow everything down—or worse, become lost. It was decided that the serum would be passed from team to team as often as possible.

The landscape of Alaska provided a natural road. Nenana was connected to the western coast of Alaska by two rivers, the Tanana and the Yukon. The first teams would follow these rivers, sledding directly on the ice whenever possible.

Detailed instructions were sent by telegraph to all the participating mushers. Each group of men and dogs was told where and when to be waiting. When the sledding team carrying the serum arrived at a transfer point, the crate of antitoxin would be moved to the new sled in mere minutes. The fresh team and musher would then speed toward the next transfer point.

Failure was unthinkable—dozens of lives were at stake!

CHAPTER THREE
Nome: Gathering the Teams

In Nome, musher Gunnar Kaasen was listening when the call for help went out. He had an experienced, powerful team, and he trusted them with his life.

He knew that Leonhard Seppala was joining the relay teams. Seppala had more reasons than most for joining in the race against time. Years before, his own daughter had caught diphtheria. Seppala had watched his little girl fight the raging fever and win. He knew what the parents in

Nome were going through. He had seen diphtheria beaten, and he was determined to see it beaten again.

Seppala had already left Nome, heading east with the best of his dogs. He had left behind many of his other dogs, including a brownish black Siberian husky named Balto.

Balto was a powerfully built, strong animal. He was very good at pulling loads on the sled. But Balto wasn't known for his great speed. In racing, Seppala relied on his fastest huskies, the ones that consistently outran all other dogs. It was these he chose to make up his team.

Gunnar Kaasen, on the other hand, thought much more highly of Balto. He had complete faith in the dog's instincts and trusted him with his life. And now there were more lives on the line.

Kaasen knew he could use Balto in his team while Seppala was away. But Balto and Kaasen couldn't help by staying in Nome. To help relay the serum, they would have to head east, where they were needed. The musher quickly volunteered to help.

Word came back almost immediately. Kaasen, Balto, and the team would be expected in Bluff, a small mining town more than sixty miles east of Nome.

Rumor had it that the first dog teams had already left Nenana and were making good time, but it was impossible to know for certain where they were. Once Balto's team reached Bluff, they would be on constant alert, as the team carrying the serum would arrive there with no warning. Balto's team would have to begin their dash to Nome with only minutes to prepare!

Gunnar Kaasen harnessed Balto and his team to the sled as swiftly as possible. He did not put Balto in the lead position.

When a musher found a good lead dog,
he worked with him as much as possible.

Kaasen knew Balto was a good dog and could pull as hard as any, but he didn't think of him as a lead dog. For the lead position, Kaasen chose a dog who had led the team many times before.

There are a number of qualities a dog must have to guide a sled and a team of dogs. A lead dog must know how to respond to commands and keep the team moving. He must be able to lead the team between trees and rocks without pulling the sled into them. He must be able to avoid sudden obstacles in the trail that the musher, on the back of the sled, cannot see.

He must be able to assert himself over the other dogs in the team, so that he is followed without question. He must be able to find and stay on the trail, no matter how bad the weather. And most important of all, a lead dog must have intuition—a natural inner knowledge of what to do. If Balto had all these skills and qualities, no one knew it—yet.

Kaasen carried a change of clothes and several lanterns, along with food for himself and the dogs. He had made the trip to Bluff many times. However, he had never made the trip with such a sense of urgency.

The streets of Nome were unusually quiet. Straining in their harnesses, eager to be on their way, the dogs seemed to understand that this was a special trip.

Balto knew what was expected of him. In the past, Kaasen had sometimes noticed Balto acting with wisdom and understanding. But Balto had never seemed more aware of what was expected of him than on this day. It was as if he knew this race would be the most important one of his life.

As Balto and the team were preparing to leave, a special health board was appointed to help deal with the growing crisis. So far, four people had died. Three of them were children. The mayor had been told that the antitoxin serum would probably reach Nome in two weeks.

Dr. Welch was not hopeful when he heard the news. Diphtheria was easy to catch. The doctor guessed that as many as eighty people might already have been exposed to it. The children who had been exposed were the ones most in danger. He could hardly bear to think what might happen to those eighty people in the two weeks they had to wait for the antitoxin.

Mushers with years of experience knew that the distance from Nenana to

Nome had been covered in less than two weeks in good weather. The record time was nine days. But these seasoned dog racers also knew the risks the relay teams were facing.

Winter had been very bad so far. It would probably get worse—colder, snowier, and icier.

Some of the dogs on the teams might even die from the effort if their mushers really pushed them. But if the mushers *didn't* push their dogs hard enough, it might be too late by the time they reached Nome.

The issue was argued back and forth as Dr. Welch worked frantically to buy his patients some time.

In the growing darkness, Kaasen turned Balto and the team toward Bluff. Setting paw after paw firmly into the snow, his muzzle high and his tail curled tightly with determination, Balto trotted into the night.

CHAPTER FOUR
Bluff, Alaska

The tiny town of Bluff wasn't much more than a few buildings near Daniel's Creek, but it was bustling with activity when Balto and the team pulled in.

Men had flocked to Bluff because black sand had been found surrounding Daniel's Creek, and people thought black sand was a sign that gold was there. But on the day Balto arrived, no one was thinking about gold. Every hope was focused on the

antitoxin serum, packed in glass vials, that was making its way westward.

Kaasen unharnessed the team and rubbed ointment into the dogs' feet. All experienced mushers know that one of their most important jobs is to take care of their animals' feet. Ice crystals can be as sharp as glass. A neglected cut on a running dog's paw can quickly become a very serious injury.

In Bluff's central building, the telegraph buzzed with news. From Nome, it was reported that the diphtheria epidemic continued to grow worse by the hour. Five people had died, and possibly over 100 people were infected. As feared, among the sickest were many children, as well as a great number of native Alaskans, also known as Inuits.

For over 10,000 years, the Inuits had lived in Alaska, hunting and fishing to survive. When Europeans first arrived in the 1700s, they brought with them diseases that the native people had no resistance to. Diphtheria and influenza were two such diseases that often took deadly tolls on the native population.

From Nenana, word had come to Bluff that a musher named Wild Bill Shannon and his team of nine dogs had picked up the serum and completed the first run of sixty miles on the Tanana River. The temperature at Shannon's departure was forty degrees below zero.

The latest news had come through on the morning of January 29, twenty hours after Shannon loaded the serum from the train onto his dogsled. Witnesses reported that the third relay team had received the serum. Led by Bill Green, the team was heading for a place called Fish Lake. There, the fourth relay team would take over and continue toward the Yukon River.

There were many small settlements along the Yukon, some equipped with telegraph equipment. Updates would continue to be sent. All reports agreed that the teams were making extremely good time.

But it was far too early to celebrate.

An inexperienced person might think that leading a dog team along the ice on a frozen river would be simple work. After all, it was a natural road, so it would be hard to get lost, and there wouldn't be trees and rocks to avoid. But mushers who had driven teams over the Yukon River knew all the problems they could run into.

For example, snow was piled high on the banks of the frozen river. A musher had no choice but to keep to the open center of the ice. There, he and the dogs were a target for the powerful Alaskan winds that swept violently down the Yukon. These winds could easily knock a man off his sled. The icy gusts could also bring temperatures down as far as sixty degrees below zero. Once the sun set, a musher ran the risk of freezing to death.

A musher also had to worry about being attacked. Alaska is home to a great variety of wildlife. There are four kinds of bears alone: grizzlies, black bears, Alaskan brown bears, and polar bears. Coyotes, wolverines, lynx, and wolves are plentiful. But one of the greatest threats to sled dogs comes from an animal that might not seem to be very dangerous—the moose.

No one knows why, but it is not unusual for a team to be ferociously attacked by a moose. Perhaps moose are unable to distinguish dogs from wolves, their natural enemies. Whatever the reason, the attacks are often deadly. A moose can come out of nowhere, leaping through the air to crush the dogs under 600 pounds of furious flesh.

Once the team has stopped, a moose uses its powerful legs and hooves to kick and slice at the animals. A musher trying to help his dogs can be injured or killed himself. Many mushers carry axes or guns with them in case of a moose attack. However, there is never a guarantee that they could get to the weapon in time.

While the men in Bluff considered these dangers, more news came—good news. Kaasen's friend and Balto's owner, the great Leonhard Seppala, was on the move with his famous racing dogs—Togo in the lead.

Seppala was headed to Nulato, a town

over 250 miles from Nome. There, he would wait for the last Yukon River team. Once the case of antitoxin reached him, he would immediately take it to Bluff, where Kaasen, Balto, and the rest of the dog team were waiting.

Curled in his bed of hay, Balto heard Seppala's name being spoken. It had not been that many years since he had been brought as a puppy to Seppala. He remembered the hours Seppala had spent training and coaching him to be a sled dog. With Gunnar Kaasen as musher, Balto had run alongside Seppala's teams at the Hammon Consolidated gold fields.

Pacing back and forth over the wooden floor, Kaasen could not even think of sleeping. He constantly went outside to see how Balto and the team were. He checked and rechecked his equipment and ran his hands over the harnesses to test for weakness. He cleaned the sled's runners until they were as slick as ice.

Balto waited patiently as Kaasen examined each of his paws, rubbing dose after dose of protective ointment into the leathery pads. Balto's patient example reminded Kaasen that he needed to eat. Once the relay team arrived, it might be many hours or even days before he would be able to rest and eat.

Amid the clicking of the telegraph and the murmur of men's voices, the lights in Bluff's wooden buildings stayed on all through the night. Each small structure acted as a beacon, lighting the way for the relay team, which might be rushing toward them under the cover of darkness.

CHAPTER FIVE
Bluff: Bad News

As the latest news came in from Nome, Balto could see the concerned looks on the men's faces. He could sense their anxiety.

Early reports of Seppala's progress turned out to be false. No one even knew where he was. Some people thought that Seppala had tried to cross the ice of Norton Sound on his way to meet the relay team, despite the fact that he had been warned that the conditions were bad.

Norton Sound pokes into the coast of

Alaska, making a wide, U-shaped inlet. The freezing waters of the Bering Sea rush in to fill the U with pack ice. Many mushers were tempted to drive across the ice instead of skirting the coast. The shortcut could take 100 miles off a journey.

But the condition of the ice was unpredictable. The wide plateau of ice was unprotected by hills or trees and gave no shelter from the wind or the blinding sun. The water beneath the ice, nudged by the currents of the Bering Sea, rose and fell.

Often, the ice moved, too. A slab of ice, with dogs and men on top, could break off from the pack and float out to sea.

Slabs could also pull apart from each other, leaving only a thin layer of newly formed ice between them. To a musher and a team of dogs, the ice would look firm until they were on top of it. Then it would be too late. Many a musher and team had plunged through thin ice and into the freezing ocean.

Most were never seen again.

CHAPTER SIX
Nome: More Bad News

As Kaasen and his dogs waited impatiently, the situation in Nome got worse.

Reports said that Dr. Welch was working around the clock and was close to collapsing from exhaustion and stress. The Nome Red Cross had organized volunteers to help the doctor, but there was only so much they could do.

There was one ray of light in all this darkness. Her name was Emily Morgan.

Nurse Emily Morgan had come from

her home in Wichita, Kansas, to do missionary work in Alaska. As luck would have it, she happened to be visiting Nome when the epidemic struck. She was a member of the Red Cross and was also a former war nurse.

During World War I, Nurse Morgan had answered the call of her country for

medical volunteers. She had served three long years overseas working with sick and wounded soldiers. No one was more qualified to handle the difficult situation in Nome. Nurse Morgan kindly agreed to stay until all of the patients were treated.

Until the antitoxin arrived, there was little the nurse and doctor could do to treat the infected patients. However, they could help to stop any further spreading of the disease.

Sleep was out of the question. The families and neighbors of the sick children had to be watched and advised carefully. Because the disease was so easy to catch, Nurse Morgan had to help families care for the sick without getting too close to them. Anyone already exposed to the disease was told to keep away from healthy people.

Despite receiving updates about the

relay teams, Nurse Morgan and Dr. Welch had no way of knowing when the serum would get to Nome. It could come in the middle of the day or in the blackness of night. But they did know it was very important to have a detailed and well-rehearsed plan of action for when it arrived.

When the antitoxin came, Dr. Welch would need help giving the shots. He and Nurse Morgan drew up a list with the names of the sickest people at the top. Most of the infected people had remained at home instead of moving to Nome's tiny hospital.

Nurse Morgan knew the address of every patient, along with his or her exact condition. She made sure she and the other volunteers would be able to get the antitoxin without delay to those who needed it most. Dr. Welch and Nurse Morgan's work keeping sick and healthy people apart seemed to be working. The infected patients were still very sick, but no new cases of diphtheria had been diagnosed for an entire day.

CHAPTER SEVEN
Norton Sound: Seppala and Togo

While Kaasen's team waited restlessly in Bluff and Nurse Morgan and Doctor Welch worked frantically in Nome, Seppala and his dog team were doing exactly what people had feared they might.

They were crossing the ice of Norton Sound.

Seppala had not made the decision to cross the sound lightly. He was well aware of the risk he was taking. But he had labored for years to develop a flawless working relationship with his dogs. He knew that the dogs understood the ice could be dangerous.

Togo—the lead dog, who had trained with Balto—had keen eyesight. His intuition was even keener. Seppala knew Togo would do his best to keep them off unstable ice.

He also knew that Togo liked to run in a perfectly straight line. This was an unusual quality, and Seppala was grateful for it. It meant that he could be certain that Togo was heading directly for the opposite shore. Togo would not go off course unless he had to.

Seppala and his team had almost crossed Norton Sound when the dogs stopped in their tracks. Seppala did not urge them on. He watched them to figure out why they had halted.

Togo had lifted his nose high into the air. His ears were pricked up. He was not behaving as if they were on unstable ice. Trusting Togo's instincts, Seppala let him pull the sled in the direction he wanted.

Soon, Seppala himself could see what Togo had discovered. Heading toward them over the ice was a team of dogs pulling a sled. On the back of the sled was a wooden crate!

Seppala had not expected to meet up with the relay team so far west. The musher driving the sled was named Henry Ivanoff. As the two men quickly moved the crate to Seppala's sled, Ivanoff filled Seppala in on what had happened so far.

It had taken seventeen relay teams to bring the serum to this point. The teams had made much better time than they had hoped. At his last checkpoint, Ivanoff had learned that a musher named Charlie Olson was waiting for Seppala in the town of Golovin.

Then Ivanoff passed on the latest news from Nome, including the number of people Dr. Welch feared were infected. He also told Seppala that he must keep the precious serum from freezing.

Filled with a new sense of urgency, Seppala turned his sled back in the direction of Nome. Again, he chose the shorter but more hazardous path—across the ice—to save time.

Togo pushed forward with all his strength.

Moments later, without warning, the dogs plunged through the ice!

CHAPTER EIGHT
Bluff, Norton Sound, and Golovin

In Bluff, Balto felt the change in the weather long before any humans. He knew a storm when he smelled one. He paced back and forth, his nose to the wind.

Kaasen thought Balto's actions came from tension and impatience, which were what Kaasen himself was feeling. He had not slept in two days. The wait was terrible.

Finally, news came.

Henry Ivanoff reported a successful

transfer to Seppala on the ice of Norton Sound. Ivanoff said that Seppala had taken off immediately and was making good time toward the town of Golovin. There, Charlie Olson and his team were waiting. High winds and blowing snow had been reported, but Olson's run to Bluff would be only thirty miles.

At last, action was close at hand!

Kaasen rechecked the sled and readied the harnesses. Balto understood his musher's actions. He leaped to his feet and stretched his muscles. They would be leaving soon!

Seppala spent several agonizing minutes on his stomach on the shattered ice with the harness lines in his hands.

He wound his feet around the sled runners to anchor himself. Then he began to get the dogs out of the water and onto firm ice.

Just one panicking dog could cause both Seppala and the sled to fall into the water. But each dog kept his head. Each dog remained calm, trusting in his musher's ability to pull him out of the freezing water. Not for the first time, Seppala was proud of his Siberian huskies.

Pulling the last shivering, wet dog from the water, Seppala looked forward to telling his friends at the Nome Kennel Club how his Siberians had remained calm in the face of disaster.

Seppala took a few minutes to rub all of the dogs' feet before going on. He knew his animals would be no worse for their icy dip as long as he took care of their paws. The dogs were protected by multiple layers of fur covering a thick layer of fat. This fur and fat made a tight seal against the frigid water and cold air.

If Seppala had fallen into the water, he would already have been suffering from severe frostbite—if the cold water itself hadn't killed him.

Seppala and his team had lost valuable time. So they continued toward the town of Golovin at a brisk pace.

They reached Golovin, and the transfer of the antitoxin to the next team was made quickly. Seppala took only a moment to warm the crate of serum by the fire. He explained to Charlie Olson that the antitoxin must not be allowed to freeze.

Olson was happy to be on his way. Golovin had been a stark reminder of what he was racing for. In 1918, an epidemic of influenza had hit the little town.

Seven years later, there were many people who had lost loved ones to the disease.

Olson did not want to see the same thing happen in Nome.

CHAPTER NINE

Bluff, Solomon, and Port Safety

Bluff was strangely silent.

It was late in the evening, and both men and dogs had eaten their fill at dinner. Once again, all of Bluff's lights were left on in the hopes that Charlie Olson's team might soon arrive.

Unknown to the people there, the weather near Nome had gotten bad. Some of the telegraph lines were down. In Bluff, it was very windy, but the conditions did not seem to be hazardous.

Balto's loud barking broke the silence.

Gunnar Kaasen heard it and rushed outside. Balto and the rest of the team were on their feet, sniffing the air. Their ears were straight and high. There could be no mistake—Olson's team must be closing in.

Sure enough, minutes later, Olson's panting dogs trotted into Bluff. Within minutes, they were surrounded by people.

Olson gave Kaasen what little information he had as Kaasen slipped his dogs into their harnesses. According to plan, Kaasen was to drive through Solomon, where there was a working telegraph, so he could get the latest news. He would then head to Port Safety, where the final musher would be waiting.

The serum was warmed and the men worked quickly, tying the crate onto

Kaasen's sled. The race hadn't been won yet. Nome was barely sixty miles away, but some difficult land lay in between.

The men gave Kaasen their good wishes, and Olson reminded him to keep the serum warm.

Balto leaned forward in his harness, straining to be on his way. He leaned, without being told, in the direction of

Nome. He remembered what they had left behind in that town and why they needed to return.

It was exactly ten o'clock at night. The temperature was dropping. With Gunnar Kaasen bringing up the rear, the team set out into the blackness, unaware of a howling blizzard that raged only miles ahead.

They were on the trail at last!

As the lead dog pulled forward, Gunnar Kaasen's eyes slowly became used to the darkness. The dogs set a quick pace after two days of waiting, and they warmed to the exercise. Gripping the handlebars of the sled as it skated over the path, Kaasen imagined what the landscape looked like in daylight. The relay was going well, but there was no room for mistakes. He wanted to be prepared for anything.

The trail to Port Safety followed the coastline, sometimes snaking out over the sea ice. This was the Seward Peninsula—the western extension of Alaska on which Nome sits. This area of Alaska is almost completely bare of trees. The landscape is harsh, rocky, and totally exposed to the elements.

Sledding at the very edge of the coast put Balto and the team in the teeth of the vicious winds sweeping in from the ocean. Kaasen had heard stories of powerful wind currents lifting entire teams of dogs off the ground. And there were other dangers, too. Kaasen had to be prepared, at any moment, to be attacked by deadly moose or other wildlife.

In the town of Solomon, the telegraph operator put a message aside for Kaasen's arrival. The message was from the Nome Board of Health, and it confirmed that a violent blizzard was raging between Solomon and Nome. The message told Kaasen and his team to stay in Solomon until the storm passed.

A message was also sent to musher Ed Rohn, who was waiting with his team at Port Safety to take over from Kaasen. Rohn was ready to take the serum the short distance remaining to Nome. But since he believed the telegraphed message meant that Balto and the team would not arrive until morning, Rohn turned out the lights and slept.

CHAPTER TEN
On the Trail

As Kaasen and his team headed west to Solomon, the wind whipped the snow into their faces. It was hard to tell where the ground began and left off. The blowing snow painted everything white. Trail, sea, and sky looked identical.

What little visibility Kaasen had had was gone. Between the darkness of night and the sheets of snow, he became disoriented. He could not see the trail at all. He wasn't sure in which direction Solomon lay. Then, to Kaasen's surprise and dismay, his lead dog stopped and refused to go on.

Nothing the musher did could get the dog to move forward. Reluctantly, Kaasen changed the dog's position and put a new animal in the lead.

That dog also refused to move. The musher had seen this sort of behavior before. He knew exactly why neither dog would lead. They could no longer pick up the trail through the high winds and blowing snow.

In other words, they were lost.

Then, in his position close to the rear, Balto strained in his harness and barked. Still crouching by the unmoving lead dog, Kaasen turned to look at Balto. He could barely see through the haze of snow, but Balto's body language was clear. *He* knew which way to go. *He* knew the trail.

Kaasen didn't waste another minute. Once the dogs realized that a new leader had picked up the trail, they would follow him without question. Kaasen unharnessed the second lead dog and put Balto in his place. Within moments, Balto was pulling the sled forward quickly and confidently.

Compared with his human musher, Balto didn't depend as much on his vision. Balto knew this trail—he knew its smells, he knew the feel of the land beneath his feet. Even in the blackest of night with snow erasing all hints of the landscape, Balto could sense the sea to his left. He could feel the rocky spread of the Topkok region to his right. He could recognize the presence of the Bonanza River several miles ahead.

Clinging to the sled, Kaasen marveled that Balto could even put one foot in front of the other.

The wind screamed into Balto's face, but he did not turn from it. Instead, he strained forward, and the dogs behind him followed his example. Balto breathed in snow along with the bitter wind, but he only pulled harder.

Kaasen was relieved. He was completely lost, but Balto was not. Though by now
Kaasen could not even see the lead dog
through the thick, blowing snow, he could
feel how confidently Balto was pulling.
With every step, Balto was sending his
musher a message—*Trust me. I'll get us
home.*

Kaasen needed no convincing. He
trusted Balto's instincts completely.

After a time, Kaasen stopped the sled
and checked each of the dogs. He found
that the blowing snow was freezing on
their eyelids. Ignoring the cold, he
crouched over each dog and gently wiped
the ice and snow from its eyes. He went to
Balto last. The lead dog was trembling,
either from strain or from his eagerness to
get going again.

Kaasen gave Balto's eyes one final rub,

then took his place on the sled. Balto could not have heard Kaasen calling commands over the howl of the storm, but he needed no direction. As soon as he sensed that Kaasen was securely on the sled, he sped forward.

In the heart of the blizzard, Kaasen never saw the buildings of Solomon to their right. The town's lights and the shapes of its buildings had been erased by the snow. Inside one of those buildings was the message for Kaasen from the Nome Board of Health telling him to wait for the blizzard to be over.

Outside, Balto and the team ran on.

CHAPTER ELEVEN
Past Port Safety

In spite of the storm, the team was making good time. Kaasen guessed they were about ten miles from Port Safety. He was hoping they would soon be safe and warm when suddenly the team came to a full stop.

Kaasen leaped off the sled. He kept one hand on the line connecting the dogs as he felt his way toward Balto. Powerful, blinding gusts of wind struck Kaasen. If he became separated from the team, he might not find his way back to them. Running his hands from one dog to the next, he found Balto standing rigid. Kaasen could not see even eight inches in front of him, so he ran his hands over his lead dog to feel for a clue.

Balto was not holding himself like a dog who had lost the trail. His body position showed that he sensed something dangerous ahead. As Kaasen ran his hands down Balto's legs, he immediately discovered the problem.

Balto was almost up to his knees in water. They were on the ice, and it had begun to give way. If Balto had taken one or two more steps, he would have gone through the ice. The dogs behind him, linked together by the harnesses, would also have gone down.

Taking Balto's harness in one hand,

Kaasen led the team around to the left and back in the direction they had come from. Once they were safely away from the broken ice, Balto leaned forward in his harness to show he was ready to go on.

Kaasen climbed back onto the sled. Balto carefully picked his way forward. After what seemed like an eternity, Kaasen felt the sled tip skyward as it was pulled up a riverbank. Balto had found secure passage over the ice. For the moment, they were safe.

Invisible to Kaasen, the trail inched closer to the sea on the team's left. The team had to pull the sled out onto the ice of Norton Sound for a short distance before reaching Port Safety. The sled now seemed to be going over a fairly flat surface, so Kaasen guessed that they might already be on the ice.

It was not smooth going.

The ice was taking a beating from the blizzard. The blowing wind was pushing it toward the barrier of the coast, forcing whole slabs up and on top of each other. Driftwood had been tossed up out of the ocean and lay everywhere. The dog team had to be very careful not to run into it.

A fierce gust of wind tossed the sled

high into the air as if it were a child's toy. Kaasen felt the sled flying for what seemed like an eternity as he clung to the handles. Finally, he landed on the ice with a sickening thud. He skidded for many feet before coming to a stop.

Still clinging to the sled, which was now on top of him, Kaasen caught his breath as Balto barked anxiously. Kaasen was shaken but not hurt. And he could tell by the sound of Balto's bark that the dogs were all right as well.

They had been very lucky.

Kaasen climbed to his feet. Then he ran his hands over the dogs' harnesses to make sure the lines were clean and untangled. Balto stood very still, understanding what needed to be done before they could go on. One of the other dogs impatiently leaped to his feet and began to pull. Balto

barked and growled at him until the dog sat down again.

While Balto kept the team in line, Kaasen carefully turned the sled over to an upright position. Checking the runners, he was relieved to find that neither of them had broken in the accident. In fact, the sled didn't seem to be damaged at all.

They could head on to Port Safety without losing any more time. The musher quickly ran his hands over the back of the sled to make sure the crate of antitoxin was still tightly tied on. The dogs tensed as Kaasen cried out in dismay.

The crate was gone!

Giving Balto a command to stay put, the musher dropped to his knees. Gripping a line leading back to the sled with one hand, he blindly felt his way over the snow and ice. He swiped furiously in the dark with his free hand. Every few seconds, he inched forward a foot or so and swept his hand in an arc through the snow.

Finally, his groping hand connected with something solid and box-like.

It was a miracle! In the midst of the

darkness and snow, Kaasen had found the crate. He dragged it back to the sled and tied it on.

The worst of their troubles was behind them. They encountered no more obstacles. Balto led purposefully, and the dogs reached incredible speeds.

The wind died down a little. Kaasen kept a lookout for Port Safety. Suddenly, he saw the Port Safety roadhouse, where he was to transfer the serum to Ed Rohn and his team.

All the lights were out.

Kaasen thought quickly. He knew that Rohn was probably at the roadhouse but asleep. Rohn could be awake and have his team in their harnesses within an hour. But every second counted, and Balto had never looked stronger or more determined. Clearly, the lead dog did not want to stop.

Nome was just over twenty miles away. Balto's confidence decided the matter. The team sped by Port Safety without a backward glance.

Several hours later, at dawn, Balto and the team thundered into Nome. Slowing the sled to a crawl on Front Street, the dogs barked and howled in celebration.

In Nome's tiny hospital, the light in Dr. Welch's office suddenly flicked on.

CHAPTER TWELVE
Nome Again

Within moments, Kaasen, Balto, and the other dogs were surrounded by well-wishers. Helping hands unharnessed the dogs and untied the crate of antitoxin. The citizens of Nome cheered Kaasen, but he kept shaking his head.

It was Balto, he kept telling them. It was Balto the whole time. Balto found the trail. Balto got them through. If it had been left to him, Kaasen said, they would still be lost in the blizzard.

Inside the hospital, the musher knelt over the crate as Dr. Welch eagerly pried it open. In spite of the accident, none of the vials were cracked or broken. Nurse Morgan had the syringes ready for the first doses of the serum.

Dr. Welch's and Nurse Morgan's expressions changed from excitement to concern when the first vial was taken out. The serum was frozen solid. They spent an anxious few minutes carefully thawing it. The serum seemed to be all right, but only time would tell.

Within the day, it became obvious that the serum had remained effective in spite of having been frozen. Up and down the streets of Nome, in their houses and in the hospital, sick children were beginning to get better. The epidemic was finally under control.

It had been just over five days since the serum had been carefully unloaded at the train station in Nenana. The entire country had followed the unfolding drama in newspaper reports. Word was triumphantly

telegraphed across the United States that the relay teams had been victorious. The children of Nome were safe at last.

PART II

CHAPTER THIRTEEN
Around the Country

Balto was the most famous dog in America. He was given a special medal. People all over the country sent requests for appearances and ceremonies.

When Leonhard Seppala got back to Nome with Togo and his team, he had mixed feelings about Balto's newfound fame. Togo had pulled Seppala's sled over 250 miles round-trip in the course of the relay. Seppala felt Togo should *also* be given some credit.

It was a difficult situation for the famous musher. He felt as if one of his children had been rewarded over another. He was extremely proud of Balto, but for the rest of his life he felt a pang of regret when he remembered how Togo's achievements had not been recognized.

On February 9, 1925, the *New York Times* ran a story that caused hearts to sink across the country. The headline read BALTO, DOG HERO OF THE DASH TO NOME, IS DEAD.

In fact, Balto was very much alive and in extremely good health. The newspaper had made an enormous mistake, reporting the death of Balto and most of the team from lung damage caused by the blizzard. The report was quickly corrected.

In Nome, Leonhard Seppala received an offer from a filmmaker who wanted to make a movie about Balto and the team. With Seppala's permission, Gunnar Kaasen took Balto and the dogs to Washington state, where the movie was filmed. There was a good deal more to come.

It seemed almost every town in America wanted Balto to pay a visit. In New York City, the unveiling of Balto's statue was scheduled for December 15, 1925. Balto and the musher traveled there for the ceremony, and Balto spent a curious moment staring at his bronze image,

which towered over the crowd.

Over the next year, Balto and the team crossed the country twice, making appearances at lecture halls and vaudeville houses alongside their musher. There was rarely an empty seat to be had when the famous dogs were onstage.

Demand was still high a year later, but it was decided the dogs needed a rest. Traveling from state to state and visiting the eager crowds was hard for the animals. It was nothing like the life they had led in Alaska. In Los Angeles, the dogs were sold

to a small museum. Reluctantly, Gunnar Kaasen returned to Alaska alone.

The dogs did not do well in Los Angeles. Balto was bewildered. The crowds were gone, and so was Kaasen. For the first time in his life, Balto did not know what was expected of him. Unhappy and uncomfortable in Los Angeles's warm climate, the dogs grew thin and sickly. They had been in the museum for over a month when a man named George Kimble, a vacationer from Cleveland, Ohio, stopped in for a visit.

Like most Americans, Kimble knew all about the heroic deeds of Balto and his team. He was horrified to see the dogs looking so unhappy. Kimble leaped into action.

Through an exchange of telegrams with friends in Cleveland, he organized a committee to raise funds to buy the dogs. They would need over $2,000. This was an enormous amount of money in 1927.

An appeal was made to the children of Cleveland. If each child donated all of his or her pennies to the fund, it might be possible to reach the goal. Across Cleveland, children emptied their piggy banks and sent their pennies in.

There wasn't much time.

Kimble needed to come up with the money within several weeks. He wasn't sure that Balto and his team's health would even hold up for that long. On the date Balto's owner said the money was due, as the last handfuls of pennies were coming in, the fund was counted.

It totaled $2,342.

CHAPTER FOURTEEN
Cleveland, Ohio

On March 27, 1927, Balto and the team arrived in Cleveland.

A new home was built for the dogs in the Brookside Zoo, which was then part of the Cleveland Museum of Natural History. There, Balto and his team were treated like royalty. Amid crowds of loving children, the dogs quickly grew fat and healthy. They got plenty of attention and food. They were also much happier in Cleveland's cooler weather.

Although they were still Alaskan sled dogs at heart, they were now seven or eight years old—middle age for a dog. They enjoyed the retirement that they had so courageously earned.

In 1933, at the age of fourteen, Balto died. It is said that one year of a dog's life is equal to seven years of a human life. This would have made Balto ninety-eight years old at the time of his death!

A stuffed mount of Balto was made. It can be seen in the Cleveland Museum of Natural History. Well over seventy years after Balto led his team and their musher into Nome, he is still captivating children and adults alike.

When Balto came to his final home in Cleveland, he completed a circle he had begun in Alaska in 1925. Then, it was the children of Nome who turned to Balto and the sled dogs for help. Two years later, when it was Balto's turn to need help, the children of Cleveland came through for the lead dog and his team.

Balto, Togo, and the hundreds of other dogs on the relay teams whose names have been forgotten are now honored. Today, visitors to the Cleveland Museum of Natural History and New York City's Central Park may come just to see Balto, or they may stumble upon him accidentally.

However they come upon the story, it is sure to stick with them—the story of dogs and children, and how they helped each other when help was needed the very most.

AFTERWORD

Every year, on the first Saturday in March, the famous Iditarod race is held. The world watches as the best dogs in Alaska retrace the route along which Balto and the relay teams pulled the antitoxin serum in 1925.

Until 1999, each Iditarod musher was greeted by Edgar Nollner, one of the original mushers of the 1925 relay, as the teams passed through the town of Galena. Nollner was twenty years old when his dogs pulled the antitoxin twenty-four miles from Whiskey Point to Galena.

Each year, he stood quietly near the Iditarod trail as the racing teams sped by. When he died in January 1999, the last participant in the great dash to Nome was gone.

Now the story is truly in the land of legends.

AUTHOR'S NOTE

It was both great fun and very frustrating to research this book on Balto. Not much has been written about this relay race to Nome, so I depended on newspaper reports that were written as the story unfolded. However, these reports were full of inconsistencies and sometimes mistakes! The sources didn't agree on exact dates and times. Even the names of towns and mushers changed from story to story. From these articles, I put together the facts as best I could.

I also read books about men and women who have raced the Iditarod with their teams. These books helped me imagine the conditions the teams would have encountered in 1925. I also learned how a dog team works and how difficult it is to be a lead dog!

Equally important were the Balto experts at the Cleveland Museum of Natural History. Some of them have spent years collecting information about the race and its aftermath. They gave me the very important story of what happened to Balto after all the excitement died down.

The story of Balto is a great one, and I hope I have done it justice.

About the Author

"I have loved both dogs and snow since I was a child," says Elizabeth Cody Kimmel. "As a little girl, I lived on a very remote road, and our house was surrounded by woods. When it snowed, I used to venture outside with our dog, my imagination creating an adventure story for us both to live. Balto's story is exactly the kind of tale I might have created—but it is true!"

Ms. Kimmel lives with her husband and daughter in Cold Spring, New York. This is her third book, and her second with a lot of snow in it.

About the Illustrator

Nora Köerber lives in Pasadena, California, with her illustrator husband, Robert Rodriguez, and their two children.

"I love illustrating children's books because there is a freedom to express feeling and mood. In *Balto and the Great Race*, I used the whirling blizzard, the ruffled fur, and the dramatic perspectives to help convey the excitement of the characters' experience."

Ms. Köerber loves animals and has two cats and one dog.

If you loved reading about Balto's
historic adventure, you won't want to
miss the incredible true story of...

The
TITANIC
SINKS!

by Thomas Conklin

A STEPPING STONE BOOK™